A HEALING JOURNAL FOR BLACK MEN

A HEALING JOURNAL FOR BLACK MEN

PROMPTS TO HELP YOU REFLECT, GROW, AND LIVE WITH PRIDE

Danny Angelo Fluker Jr.

callisto
publishing
an imprint of Sourcebooks

Copyright © 2022 by Callisto Publishing LLC
Cover and internal design © 2022 by Callisto Publishing LLC
Interior and Cover Designer: Jill Lee
Art Producer: Maya Melenchuk
Editor: John Makowski
Production Editor: Cassie Gitkin
Production Manager: David Zapanta

Published by Callisto Publishing LLC C/O Sourcebooks LLC
P.O. Box 4410, Naperville, Illinois 60567-4410
(630) 961-3900
callistopublishing.com

Printed and bound in the United States of America
VP 3

This
journal
belongs to:

_____

_____

CONTENTS

Introduction *viii*

How to Use This Journal *x*

SECTION 1: Reflect on Who You Are *1*

SECTION 2: Acknowledge Your Pain *29*

SECTION 3: Treat Yourself with Kindness *57*

SECTION 4: Dare to Think Positively *85*

SECTION 5: Take Care of Your Whole Self *113*

SECTION 6: Step into Your Power *141*

Rest in Yourself; Celebrate You *168*

Resources *170*

References *172*

INTRODUCTION

Mindfulness, meditation, and yoga are all practices I chose to lessen the impact of anxiety and depression in my life. Over time, the feelings of deep sadness about the past and active worry about the future became smaller and took up a lot less energy in my mind and body. I fell in love with wellness practices and the history behind them. That began for me a journey dedicated to being a lifelong student of wellness practice.

As Black males, healing requires us to face the residual impact of historical, cultural, communal, and systematic effects on our person. Black people throughout the diaspora share a communal memory of terror, and generations of multiple cultures dispersed and evolved from specific injuries of the past. These injuries were with our forebears in their present, and in many ways those injuries reveal themselves in our present as well. By facing the residual impact of harm, we acknowledge those things within ourselves that are not in stillness and peace and work with them through modalities that bring about alleviation and reprieve.

I became a mindfulness and meditation instructor and a yoga teacher. My yoga training first focused on fitness and grew to focus on brain science and the relationship of the human nervous system with yoga tradition. I've taught thousands of students and created an organization that focuses on the emotional, mental, and physical well-being of Black boys and Black men. We do this by holding educational spaces for Black males to explore mindfulness, meditation, and yoga, virtually and in person, through a communal network of Black male instructors around the globe. It's been encouraging to be in these community spaces and to see how necessary it is for those who identify as male in our communities to breathe and be.

Part of my wellness also involved being initiated into the Missoko Bwiti tradition of my paternal ancestors in Gabon, Africa. Bwiti is an oral, indigenous African path, native to tribes in Gabon. Bwiti is also a spiritual practice of individual and communal knowing. For thousands of years, Bwiti has been used in communal ritual life, for connection to ancestors and for healing. As an American descendant of chattel slavery, this was an integral part of my own journey of discovery and deep healing.

Since an early age, journaling has been a method of remembering and honoring my life journey. While journaling, I reflected on what life was communicating to me and I learned to be kind to myself in the process. Journaling opens space to explore and express our inner world. It is a powerful tool used by many great Black men, including Malcolm X, Nelson Rolihlahla Mandela, Dr. Martin Luther King Jr., James Baldwin, President Barack Hussein Obama, and others. The affirmations, prompts, exercises, and practices in this journal will encourage going deep within our Blackness, along with sharing practical daily practice and our healing dance together. We hold a conscious collective memory of shared experiences from our communities and ancestors across the diaspora. Greatness is in our embodiment. Masculine energy is at our core. The greatness of multiple cultures across Africa and our collective diaspora embraces us each in our connection with ourselves, our communities, and humanity as a whole. This journal is for all Black men regardless of whether you are cisgender, transgender, transmasculine, nonbinary, gender nonconforming, male socialized, and/or masculine of center.

This journal will be a tool to reflect and document your unique lived experiences. Try different practices and affirmations, and breathe in expansion and self-compassion. If you experience persistent anxiety or depression, give yourself permission to seek the support of a mental health professional. There are communities of Black professional healers that exist to support us. I've listed a few organizations in the resources section of this book.

My hope is that this journal will be a touch point for your own journey in discovering what wholeness and well-being mean for you. Finding ways to come home to ourselves is what healing often is. When we breathe in the gift of life, we also breathe in possibilities for ourselves of which we aren't even aware. We breathe in boundless good that we have and haven't imagined. As you work through this journal, celebrate yourself for choosing your own well-being.

HOW TO USE THIS JOURNAL

The guided prompts, affirmations, practices, and exercises of this book are designed to be practical and accessible. Explore the sections that resonate most with you. Some practices may feel best at different times and even seasons. Flow with what works. Tap into the natural rhythms of each day. What time of day do you find is best to journal? Mornings may be filled with ritual and intention setting. Midday may be a good break with time to be still and remember. Evenings may be good for decompression and reflection. You will move through different energies on different days. Honor all those energies. Honor all of you.

This journal has six sections, focusing on identity, processing emotions, self-compassion, positive thinking, self-confidence, and pride. Prompts will have open-ended questions that will allow space for you to explore as you write. Affirmations are to remind you of your power. Practices are things you can do when you aren't journaling. Exercises will involve writing in your journal in specific guided ways. You don't have to work through these journal pages from front to back. Take into consideration your time, what you want to work through, and your varying needs.

You are invited to go all in with this journal. Give yourself permission to go deep and see what you find for yourself and for what you create as you move through the pages. You are what makes this journal special. There is no other you. My goal in these pages is to be a guide into your own seeing of your fullness, light, and enoughness.

SECTION 1

REFLECT ON WHO YOU ARE

Seeing the fullness of what makes you *you* is a gift. Your uniqueness is unmatched. The space you take up in the world and in life is invaluable. What you connect with, the experiences that have formed your identity, and what you acknowledge as true for yourself are all part of the reflections of who you are. Deeper self-reflection is in self-awareness. Self-awareness is a window inside yourself. Vulnerability and honesty work together with self-awareness because in being real with what is, there is personal power. Inward knowing also helps with being present in the moment. Being present in the moment is the heart of mindfulness. Mindfulness asks that you meet life in a gentle and open way as it unfolds over and over again. Truthfulness and self-acceptance are good practices when looking inside. Here are tools to cultivate self-awareness as you reflect on who you are.

EVERYTHING I AM
IS ENOUGH.

Reflect on all that you are. What are three things you can affirm as authentic to you? How do these three things show up in your everyday life? What do you value most about each of these three things?

_____

_____

_____

_____

_____

_____

_____

_____

_____

_____

_____

_____

_____

_____

_____

Think of a time when you felt complete, accomplished, or enough. Describe what it felt like. How did it feel to be enough during that time? What can you commit to in your life to ensure you feel enough, complete, and accomplished more often?

_____

_____

_____

_____

_____

_____

_____

_____

_____

_____

_____

_____

_____

_____

_____

_____

_____

_____

Self-Referral Quiz

Self-referral helps tap into self-awareness and mindfulness. Answer the following questions in ways that are authentic to your lived experience.

1. Who am I?

\
\

2. What does identity mean to me?

\
\

3. What experiences in my life have made me who I am today?

\
\

4. How often do I take time to reflect on who I am?

\
\

5. How can I make more time throughout my day for self-reflection?

\
\

Self-Referral and Body Scan

This mindfulness practice aims to get to the heart of who you are, with stillness, breath, and inquiry into the inner workings of personal awareness.

1. Find a quiet, open space, and if it's comfortable for you, lie flat on your back. (If you are unable to lie on your back, find a comfortable place to sit upright.)

2. Place one hand on your heart and one hand on your belly.

3. Give yourself five to ten minutes to just be, breathing slow, deep, even breaths.

4. Ask internally, "Who am I?" See what comes up and be with it.

5. Notice your heartbeat under one hand and the rise and fall of your belly under the other hand.

6. Send gratitude to your heart and breath.

7. Send gratitude to your body and your being.

8. Continue to breathe and rest right where you are, for as long as you desire, unapologetically.

How can you confirm for yourself that you are enough, just as you are? What are some things you can think, say, or do to remind you of your enoughness? What would it take to create a day, routine, and life habit that reminds you of your enoughness?

Oftentimes you may see reflections in media and culture that state that who you are as an individual is not enough. They suggest there are things external to yourself that you must acquire or become to be enough. Why is feeling enough necessary? What does being enough right now mean?

_____

_____

_____

_____

_____

_____

_____

_____

_____

_____

_____

_____

_____

_____

_____

_____

_____

What does Blackness mean to you? What does masculinity mean to you? How are Blackness and masculinity expressed in your everyday life? What do you value most about your Blackness and masculinity?

I SEE AND ACCEPT
ALL OF ME.

The brain has over a quadrillion synapses, and the number of brain states is one followed by a million zeroes. Navigation of different brain states determines how you show up in the world. What do you value most about how your mind works?

_____

_____

_____

_____

_____

_____

_____

_____

_____

_____

_____

_____

_____

_____

_____

Understanding your relationship to success also relates to your sense of worth and identity. How do you define success? How has your understanding of success changed over time? What are some of your personal successes? Do you attach these personal successes to who you are? Why or why not?

Three Circles Map

This exercise gives space for writing out and visually identifying the intangible parts of your inner world in how you relate to yourself and your desires. Visualization is a mindful tool for the creation and execution of the things that you are adding into the world.

   Fill up each of the three circles below with as much as you can. The My Passions circle is meant for those things that light up your heart. The Authentically Me circle should be filled with things that are unique to who you are as an individual. The My Dreams circle is meant to hold the things you desire for your life.

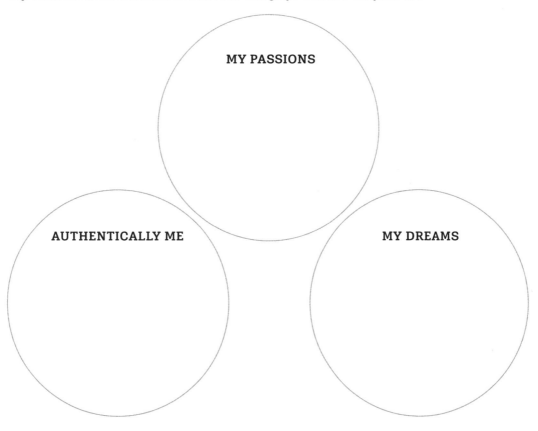

I GIVE MYSELF PERMISSION
TO JUST BE.

Four Practice

This meditation focuses on four specific things: breath, being, presence, and gratitude. You can always focus on these four things at any given moment throughout your day, no matter what you are doing. The Four Practice is grounding and centering, and it reduces tension in the mind and body.

1. Set a timer on your phone, ideally for five to ten minutes.

2. Allow yourself to be completely comfortable, positioning your body where and how you desire.

3. Begin focusing on your breath. You don't have to breathe a certain way; just take notice that you are breathing.

4. Bring your attention from your breath to things in your life for which you are deeply grateful.

5. Bring your awareness to the present moment. Pay attention to the sensations of your body as you do something specific, such as tap your thumb across each finger or hum.

6. Become still in your body with deep, even breaths, and notice the subtle energies within and around you.

Community, family, and your connection to others shape your sense of identity. How do you show up in your relationships with friends, family, colleagues, and/or romantic partners? Why is it important for you to show up to each of these relationships in this way?

Reflecting on your accomplishments reveals the ways in which your identity has shaped the pivotal moments in your life. What milestones in life are you most proud of? How has your life changed because of these milestones? What part of your identity contributed to making these steps possible?

Dedication to something bigger than yourself speaks to personal mission and purpose, and is also a reflection of your values. What in life do you hold sacred, and why? Reflect on your commitment. Journal about how dedication to this higher ideal is of personal value to you.

_____

_____

_____

_____

_____

_____

_____

_____

_____

_____

_____

_____

_____

_____

_____

_____

I GIVE KINDNESS
TO EVERY PART OF ME.

Your culture bathes you with food, expression, customs, and ways of seeing and being in the world. What are some things in your culture that you celebrate for the joy of being part of it? How is culture related to your identity?

_____

_____

_____

_____

_____

_____

_____

_____

_____

_____

_____

_____

_____

_____

What is your heritage? What are tangible and intangible things that have been passed down to you in your family, and what do you value most about these things? How does your heritage relate to your sense of self?

_____

_____

_____

_____

_____

_____

_____

_____

_____

_____

_____

_____

_____

_____

_____

My Mantra

Mantras are empowering statements of affirmation and belief. They are a useful tool for positively reinforcing thoughts, ideas, and mental patterns. If you think about the negative impact of worry and rumination on the nervous system, imagine mantras doing the exact opposite. You activate the reward centers of the brain rather than the cortisol or stress-producing responses within the body.

1. Take some time to create a mantra of your own (e.g., "I do good things and good things return to me"). Make your mantra twenty-five words or less.

2. Write your mantra twenty-five times in one sitting.

3. Say the mantra (aloud or quietly to yourself) each time that you write it.

4. Commit to conducting your mantra-writing exercise twice a day.

Sit and Breathe

The benefits of this practice include the downregulation of the nervous system, reducing stress, and producing feelings of calm. Mindfulness helps with practicing presence with what is both in the body and the environment. Give yourself permission to sit and breathe.

1. Make yourself comfortable. Give yourself enough space to take whatever shape your body wants in a supported way.

2. For any length of time you desire, sit down and allow yourself to pay attention to your breathing.

3. Honor every thought and emotion that arises. See and feel them, and bring your attention back to your breathing.

4. Observe your breath and see if you can match the length of your inhales with the length of your exhales.

5. When you are ready to get up, bring some gentle movement to your body.

Ancestry is a map showing your journey in the tapestry of humanity. Many hold to ancestry as an anchor for their own sense of being. Is ancestry important to you? Why or why not? Who are your ancestors? How does your relationship and understanding of your ancestry impact your sense of self?

Community creates a sense of belonging and shapes individual lives. What does it mean to you? How has community shaped your sense of identity? What role does it play in your life currently and how do you show up for the things you value in community?

How would you describe your sense of self? What makes you, you? What qualities can you name that are deeper than life experience, possessions, titles, and work? Why is a sense of self necessary and important in navigating the world? How do you protect your sense of self?

_____

_____

_____

_____

_____

_____

_____

_____

_____

_____

_____

_____

_____

_____

_____

_____

I PROTECT MY HAPPINESS
WITH CONSISTENCY IN THINGS
I ENJOY AND BOUNDARIES
FOR MY CHOICES.

SECTION 2

ACKNOWLEDGE YOUR PAIN

It's okay to feel, and feel deeply. Feeling is part of the human experience. Experiencing the broad range of your emotions is part of your emotional and mental health. Your feelings speak to you. Excitement has one voice; sadness and pain have another. To be aware of pain is being with the voice and discomfort of pain in your mind and body. Being with the pain, honoring it as valid, and allowing the energy of the pain to be moved are part of processing the pain. Processing your various emotions gives space for observation and self-compassion.

Elements in this section focus on awareness of your pain, being with the pain, and working through pain. Practices will center on being with the emotions in your body in gentle ways. Prompts will focus on questions to explore areas of past and possible present pain. Exercises will examine ways to work through the emotion of pain.

**THE HURT I'M EXPERIENCING
IS REAL. I DON'T LIKE IT,
AND THAT'S OKAY.**

What is something that has caused pain in your life? Write out the type of pain. (Examples include grief, betrayal, anger, and heartbreak.) Breathe deeply as you write and reflect. Challenge yourself to not hold back in expressing what it is you experienced. Be patient with yourself as you reflect.

_____

_____

_____

_____

_____

_____

_____

_____

_____

_____

_____

_____

_____

_____

_____

_____

_____

_____

Write about three past scenarios in which you experienced pain. What type of pain did you experience in each circumstance (physical, emotional, mental)? You might find that experiences overlap. Write freely and honestly about each instance.

Checklist of Experiences with Pain

In this exercise, you will go through a checklist of several types of pain that you may have felt or may be feeling. Check off the ones you know well and write a short note about your experience with each.

☐ Anger

_____

_____

_____

☐ Grief

_____

_____

_____

☐ Sadness

_____

_____

_____

☐ Worry

_____

_____

_____

Savasana (Corpse Pose)

In this practice you will explore an intentional resting yoga posture, which brings the body into a state of homeostasis and downregulates your nervous system. This resting state is *savasana*, Sanskrit for "corpse posture." In this state, you give yourself permission to do nothing and just be. You might fall asleep, which is normal.

1. Find a quiet, open space where you can be comfortable.

2. Set a timer with a soft alert for ten to fifteen minutes.

3. Allow yourself to lie flat on your back with your limbs extended comfortably and open. Try to soften and relax every area of your body with smooth, even breathing as you lie.

4. You are welcome to close your eyes or have a softly focused gaze.

5. Be gentle coming out of your yogic sleep; start with small movements like tapping your thumb across each finger or rotating your wrists.

6. When the timer goes off, or when you are ready to be done, come to your side and slowly bring yourself up to a seated position.

What are some ways in which your embodied pain might be unique to your experience as a Black, masculine individual? If there is uniqueness to pain as a Black male, why do you think that is? Why is acknowledging the pain of the Black male experience important?

Is pain necessary in the human experience? Why or why not? What has been your personal experience when thinking about whether pain is something that is needed as a part of life?

_____

_____

_____

_____

_____

_____

_____

_____

_____

_____

_____

_____

_____

_____

In this present moment, what is your relationship to pain? Are you close or far away? What are some contrasts you notice between where you are now and pain you experienced prior to this moment?

I GIVE MYSELF PERMISSION
TO FEEL MY ANGER DEEPLY
WITHOUT APOLOGY.
MY ANGER IS VALID.

In your experience of pain, what are some insights that you were able to carry with you beyond your experience of the pain? What are some lessons and wisdom you have gained from your pain? Have these insights been able to help you in other circumstances in life?

What does grief mean to you? Recall a time in your life when you experienced the pain of grief. What were the circumstances that led to your experience of that grief? What are some things that you can allow yourself to sit with when you think about that time?

_____

_____

_____

_____

_____

_____

_____

_____

_____

_____

_____

_____

_____

_____

_____

_____

_____

_____

Free-Form Doodling

The purpose of this exercise is to feel intuitively and to allow those feelings to move your hand through creative expression in doodling or writing. This free-form scribbling will be another means by which you can move energy through the pages of this journal.

1. Take a few moments to sit with how you are feeling and the energies present where you are in the moment.

2. Bring your pen tip to the space below and, if it's comfortable for you, close your eyes.

3. Take three deep, smooth breaths and begin to move your pen across the paper in whichever way feels natural to you. Continue for as long as you desire.

4. See if you can still move your pen in a way that is guided by what you feel rather than what you think you should be doing.

I HONOR EVERY PART
OF MY ANGER WHILE ALSO
HONORING EVERY PART OF ME.

Breath Work

This breathing technique allows the movement of energy through the body, moving in waves through consistent breathing. It uses the power of the breath and can result in an increase of energy and the ability to move through difficult emotions.

1. Find a quiet place where you can sit or stand comfortably.

2. Begin by noticing your breathing. Pay close attention to the quality of your inhales and exhales, and notice where in the body the air is concentrated.

3. When you are ready, begin to inhale and exhale through the mouth.

4. Take smooth, even inhales and exhales, back-to-back.

5. Continue back-to-back inhales and exhales, making your exhale just a little bit longer than your inhale now, even if it's just a beat.

6. Repeat for as long as is comfortable; try twenty to forty-five seconds to start.

7. When you are ready to finish this practice, allow yourself to return to the natural rhythms of your breath, breathing as you normally would.

What does anger mean to you and what is your experience with it? How have you expressed, kept in, or explored your anger in the past? What does anger feel like in your mind, body, and energy? What is one time you felt significant anger, and what did you take away from that experience?

_____

_____

_____

_____

_____

_____

_____

_____

_____

_____

_____

_____

_____

_____

_____

_____

_____

What is your relationship to pain in your body? Sometimes emotional pain can manifest in the physical body. What does physical pain mean to you? What are some things you have found to help you in your relationship to physical pain?

What does trust mean to you and what is your relationship to it? What does betrayal mean to you? What does betrayal mean to you? Have you ever experienced betrayal? If so, what did that feel like in your mind and body? What happened in your experience and what did you take away from it?

_____

_____

_____

_____

_____

_____

_____

_____

_____

_____

_____

_____

_____

_____

_____

_____

_____

I RESPOND TO MY PAIN'S VOICE THE BEST I CAN, EVEN IF THAT RESPONSE IS DOING NOTHING.

Have you ever experienced pain because of being in close relationships with others? What did the pain feel like in your heart and body? What does heartbreak mean to you, and what were some things you did at the time to move through that heartbreak? What gifts, if any, did you receive from the pain of heartbreak?

_____

_____

_____

_____

_____

_____

_____

_____

_____

_____

_____

_____

_____

_____

_____

_____

_____

When you think about pain, what is its opposite? Reflect on what the opposite of pain is in your lived experience and write down moments when you felt and embodied the opposite of pain. What was that like? What made these experiences of the opposite of pain distinct from past experiences of pain?

Your Lived Experience

Consider the list of words below relating to types of pain and other emotions. Write about what each word means to you, based on your lived experience.

TYPES OF PAIN/ EMOTIONS	YOUR DEFINITION AND LIVED EXPERIENCE
Despair	
Feeling Misunderstood	
Heartbreak	
Loss	
Feeling Overwhelmed	
Feeling Powerless	

Somatic Tapping

In this practice, you will explore tapping your body with your hands and fingers, moving across different areas of your body. Repeatedly tapping your fingers on specific areas of the body creates a dialogue between the brain and the area of the body being engaged, often reducing tension and stress.

1. Make yourself comfortable. You can sit, stand, or lie on your back.

2. Bring the tips of your fingers from both hands toward your forehead and upper face. Using the pads at the tips of your fingers, tap repeatedly in a way that feels natural to you, ensuring you have a lightness in your wrist.

3. As you tap, breathe smooth, even breaths.

4. Move your tapping to the sides of your face, the top of your head, and your neck.

5. Allow your tapping to continue, this time covering areas of your body that you feel intuitively called to tap.

6. Continue tapping for a minute or more wherever feels natural, breathing consistently.

7. Take note of how you feel as you tap, and cease whenever you feel ready.

When might pain be helpful to you? Consider a time when pain might have changed something in your life in a positive way. This might be something that wasn't evident at the time but was clear later.

As you have explored a deeper understanding of the "voice" of pain, write a scenario in which you have a conversation with it. What would you say to pain? What questions would you ask pain? What other emotions might you express in your conversation with pain?

_____

_____

_____

_____

_____

_____

_____

_____

_____

_____

_____

_____

_____

_____

_____

_____

_____

_____

Write a brief note to yourself about your understanding of pain in all its various forms. Encourage yourself in that letter—give pointers, warnings, and whatever else is on your heart as you write. As you write, think about different timelines in your life. Shift between your present, past, and future selves.

BEING WITH MY PAIN IS ENOUGH;
I DON'T HAVE TO TRY TO
MAKE IT GO AWAY BEFORE
ITS TIME TO PASS.

SECTION 3

TREAT YOURSELF WITH KINDNESS

Caring for yourself begins with the compassion you give yourself in any given moment. Opportunities for self-compassion are everywhere. They include: awareness of your inner dialogue, or the things you say to yourself that no one else hears; grace when things don't go as planned or when a mistake is made; and proactively engaging in gratitude for being exactly who you are. Kindness is a constant—despite life's changes—that ensures you are moving through the day with self-compassion. Living in kindness toward yourself honors your inherent value and can also be a means to uplift your spirit, energy, and mood. Being kind to yourself also provides clarity in daily tasks and feelings of deep connection with yourself and others. Prompts in this section will explore questions around kindness. Practices in this section will be reminders of ways to operate out of a place of inner kindness. Exercises will explore kindness.

I CHOOSE KINDNESS FOR MYSELF.
KINDNESS TOWARD MYSELF
IS MY METHOD OF HEALING.

What does your internal dialogue feel like? Consider the words, tone, and energy behind your self-talk. Do you think it's important to feel a certain way when considering how you interact with yourself internally? Why might it be important to feel one way or another?

_____

_____

_____

_____

_____

_____

_____

_____

_____

_____

_____

_____

_____

_____

_____

_____

_____

Write down your definition of kindness. As you write, consider moments in which you have received the kindness of another and have shown kindness to another. See if you can also tap into the feeling of kindness as you reflect.

_____

_____

_____

_____

_____

_____

_____

_____

_____

_____

_____

_____

_____

_____

_____

_____

_____

_____

Kind Mind

This exercise will explore various types of internal dialogue and emotions in your mind. The goal is to uncover new ways in which self-kindness can emerge.

1. In the open space below, write down five things that you say to yourself when you are feeling down, make a mistake, or when you're not feeling like yourself.

2. Note how this internal dialogue makes you feel in addition to the feelings that are already present.

3. In the second open space below, write five things that you can say kindly to yourself in place of the original internal dialogue in the same circumstance.

4. Write down the way you desire to feel because of this new affirming internal dialogue.

Your Celebration Playlist

This practice is an intentional act of choosing to champion the self and is a heightened expression of self-kindness. Self-kindness will be expressed through the joy of movement and by the release of dopamine, the happiness chemical, in the brain, encouraged through good music and vibrations.

1. Set aside time to create a celebratory playlist. Using your favorite music app or music platform, choose a minimum of five songs (or vibrations) that speak to your joy, reflect your lived experience, or that particularly resonate with you.

2. Schedule fifteen to twenty minutes for joyful movement.

3. Listen to the music, feel the vibrations, and allow yourself to celebrate all that you are as an act of kindness. Envision this as time set aside just for you.

4. Make this a ritual. Schedule time to enjoy celebratory movement as something you do once a week or several times a month.

Think of a recent time when you have experienced kindness. What were the circumstances surrounding the experience and how did it make you feel? What about the experience did you understand as kind, and why was the experience of value to you?

Think of a deliberate act of kindness that you can do for someone this week. Is it possible for you to call or visit someone? Could you send a gift or display a warm smile? Write out your plan to show kindness to someone and set an intention to accomplish it. How might planning these acts be reflective of your own self-kindness?

Think of your most recent inner dialogue about yourself. Was it kind? Write some things that you could say to yourself in the future that might be more kind or might expand on the kindness that you've already given yourself.

_____

_____

_____

_____

_____

_____

_____

_____

_____

_____

_____

_____

_____

_____

_____

_____

_____

SELF-COMPASSION IS
MY STRENGTH AND THE
GUARDIAN OF MY PEACE.

Brainstorm a few kind things to plan for yourself. What can you commit to doing over the next few days that's deliberately kind to yourself? What would you enjoy? What would feel good? Write about this below. Make a list of at least five kind things and your plan for doing each.

What are your beliefs and conditioning around the necessity for self-kindness? Why is being kind to yourself necessary? When reflecting on your own experience, why is it important to be kind to yourself? Journal about two ways self-kindness is important.

_____

_____

_____

_____

_____

_____

_____

_____

_____

_____

_____

_____

_____

_____

_____

_____

_____

Love Letter to the Soul

This exercise will explore the power of calling your energy, love, purpose, and kindness back to yourself for the purpose of elevating your felt sense of well-being and increasing self-kindness.

1. Take some time to reflect on who you are beyond any outside expectation or responsibility.

2. In the open space below, write a love letter to yourself. Express what you value most about your essence and write out your truest desires and goals. What would you do if the impossible had no power?

3. Write about your desire for self-kindness and fully express deep care for your well-being and hopes for all that you are.

4. Tap into affirmation, self-kindness, and fearlessness, and express that to yourself without apology.

I AM WORTHY OF MY
GREATEST KINDNESS. I DESERVE
MY GREATEST KINDNESS.

Self-Kindness through Observation

The purpose of this practice is to cultivate a sense of intimacy, mindfulness, and intentional presence with oneself. Paired with attention to the breath and kind dialogue, this practice can cause deep emotion and feelings of centeredness, calm, and well-being.

1. Choose a time when you have a quiet environment to yourself, and stand in front of a mirror.

2. Close your eyes and allow yourself ten to twenty deep, even breaths with your hand on your heart.

3. Open your eyes and gaze directly into the eyes of your reflection. Stare deeply without intentional thought at first.

4. Simply be with your gaze, breathing even, smooth inhales and exhales.

5. Continuing to gaze at your reflection, send yourself a smile through your eyes and the feeling of gratitude.

6. Tell yourself kind things internally or aloud.

7. Breathe deeply and stay with your gaze.

8. Take all the time you need. When you are ready to be finished, take a long, slow, cleansing breath in, and release it as you disengage your self-gaze.

What are some challenges you have faced and may have been hard on yourself about? What was your inner dialogue like in those moments and what were some ways in which you were not kind to yourself during that time? What can be done differently with how you treat yourself in present and future challenges?

_____

_____

_____

_____

_____

_____

_____

_____

_____

_____

_____

_____

_____

_____

_____

_____

How do you manage kindness with others? Journal about times when you showed kindness to others and how they received it. How does your kindness with others match, exceed, or fall short of your kindness toward yourself?

How do behaviors and emotions factor into self-kindness? How have some emotions you've experienced and behaviors you've expressed pair with self-kindness? What are some things you can do to help with emotional and behavioral self-kindness?

**SELF-KINDNESS IS A GIFT
I HAVE THE POWER TO GIVE
MYSELF AT ANY MOMENT.**

What are some mistakes you have made? How did those mistakes make you feel? What did your internal dialogue about those mistakes look like? Was there room to be more kind to yourself in that dialogue? What behaviors would have helped you practice self-kindness in those moments?

_____

_____

_____

_____

_____

_____

_____

_____

_____

_____

_____

_____

_____

_____

_____

_____

Think of times when you knew that you recognized your value and that you were in alignment in honoring yourself with good energy and gratitude. Journal about moments when you felt good about self-kindness. How can you intentionally invite more of those moments into your life?

Self-Kindness through Reflection

Set aside some time to explore statements of self-kindness. There is space provided at the end of each statement for you to complete each thought. Write what resonates most with you.

Self-kindness helps me throughout the day by

_____

_____

I value myself enough to be kind to myself because

_____

_____

My quality of mind and life are improved by self-kindness because

_____

_____

Finding stillness and presence with my internal dialogue is important because

_____

_____

Because of self-kindness I gain

_____

_____

Walking and Gratitude Meditation

This practice combines movement, gratitude, and mindfulness. You will explore tapping into the energy of gratitude as you intentionally walk or move in a way that feels good for you. Mindfulness brings the mind to the present moment and can bring about feelings of stillness and calm, and gratitude can uplift your mood.

1. Create a list of things that you are grateful for.

2. Organize the list into a mantra, or a statement that can be easily remembered and repeated.

3. Set a course for intentional joyful movement in nature and begin to focus on the things you are grateful for.

4. Tap into what gratitude feels like in your mind and body as you move.

5. Pair your reflections of gratitude with the breath and intentional feeling.

Some days can be hard, and things may not go the way you planned or hoped. Your energy may be low. You might be discouraged, not feel like yourself, or not want to do any of the things that you had originally set out to do. How does self-kindness relate to those moments in the day that aren't desirable?

What role does self-kindness have in relation to Black male identity? Oftentimes you may see images or hear about and experience things that are far from kind. What are some ways you can counteract negativity that comes as the result of someone or something else's unkindness toward you? Why might it be even more important to celebrate all that you are in the face of unkindness?

What does joy rooted in celebration of yourself look and feel like? When have you ever celebrated yourself unapologetically? What was the root of that celebration? When might you do it again or begin to celebrate yourself if you haven't already?

_____

_____

_____

_____

_____

_____

_____

_____

_____

_____

_____

_____

_____

_____

_____

_____

I AM KIND TO ALL THAT
I HAVE BEEN, ALL THAT I AM,
AND ALL THAT I WILL BE.

SECTION 4

DARE TO THINK POSITIVELY

Positive thinking doesn't mean that everything is okay; sometimes life isn't okay. Positive thinking is controlling your inner narrative so that life can be faced in a way where there is nothing you can't overcome. It takes courage to think in ways that are uplifting, and courage is found in gratitude for what is, and in joyful hope for the future. Sometimes, cultivating a positive mindset comes from wellness practices, therapy, medication, or a combination of each. The journal elements in this section will focus on wellness practices, with the aim of being true to what you feel and experience, while opening space for the possibility of positivity.

I CHOOSE GRATITUDE
AND JOY FOR MYSELF AND
MY WELL-BEING. I EMBRACE
ACCEPTANCE AND FLOW IN LIFE.

Would you consider your outlook and mindset to be positive? What are words or phrases that describe your mindset on a typical day? How has your mindset changed over time? What would it take to maintain or develop a positive mindset?

What does having a positive mindset and outlook mean to you? How would you describe thinking positively in your own words? What has been your experience with the stories and reflections of your mind? Do you find that you must actively encourage yourself? Why or why not?

_____

_____

_____

_____

_____

_____

_____

_____

_____

_____

_____

_____

_____

_____

_____

_____

Thought Watch

Actively practicing the watching of your thoughts and feelings allows you to find a sense of centeredness and responsibility. Use the blank chart in this exercise to document your thoughts throughout the course of the day. Doing so will allow you to assess whether your thoughts are part of a personal positive outlook. An example is included below:

EARLY MORNING	AFTERNOON	EARLY EVENING	LATE EVENING
I'm feeling a bit overwhelmed.	*I feel light and hopeful about my tasks.*	*I feel grateful with how things went today.*	*Life is good.*
Reflections:	**Reflections:**	**Reflections:**	**Reflections:**

EARLY MORNING	AFTERNOON	EARLY EVENING	LATE EVENING
Reflections:	**Reflections:**	**Reflections:**	**Reflections:**

Thought Watch Meditation

Thought watch meditation is a practice of watching the different paths and patterns of thoughts as you meditate. Thought meditation is good for centering, calming the mind, and increasing presence and inward control. Watching each thought in observation and not absorption is the goal.

1. Find a quiet place of seclusion.

2. Set a timer on your phone for your desired length of meditation (try five minutes to start).

3. Close your eyes or find a focal point for a soft gaze.

4. Begin your meditation with smooth, even breathing.

5. As you breathe, notice the thoughts that enter your head without getting attached to them.

6. Listen to the conversations of your mind without identifying with or concentrating on any particular thought.

7. Breathe with intention and observation while watching each thought.

8. Bring your attention to your breath and bring your attention to awareness for as long as you can.

9. When the timer goes off, take several moments to bring yourself back into active awareness of your body and environment through gentle, intentional movements.

Recall a time when you felt you had a particularly positive mindset and outlook. What life circumstances were you experiencing? What did your workflow, creativity, and relationships look like? What is one memory that you favor most from that time? Is there anything that you can do to closely replicate that positive mindset and outlook into your current daily life?

There are circumstances in life that don't feel good and can even be discouraging. Recognize the moments in which you might not feel your best, and that acceptance of your thoughts and feelings is helpful for your mental health. How do you care for your mental health presently?

You might not feel your best at a particular moment, and that's okay. Positivity is rooted in acceptance, and you may find that you are closer to a helpful mindset even in moments when you might not feel like yourself. Why is acceptance of life as it is important?

MY MIND IS A TOOL FOR
MY BENEFIT. I FILL IT WITH
THINGS THAT UPLIFT
AND ENCOURAGE ME.

What does positivity feel like to you? Think about your energy, mind, and body. What can you accomplish when feeling this way? What do you believe is possible when feeling positive? What are some ways you can invite more of that feeling into your life?

Engaging your thoughts in healthy ways impacts your outlook. Positivity can sometimes mean optimism and embracing the good qualities of something. How do you typically approach different narratives in your thoughts? What are some healthy ways in which you can engage your thoughts?

_____

_____

_____

_____

_____

_____

_____

_____

_____

_____

_____

_____

_____

_____

_____

_____

_____

Mantra Creation

The repetition of a mantra aids in concentration and can put energy and intention toward something desired. The goal of this exercise is to take some time to write out a specific word and its meanings and to create an affirming statement that can be repeated as desired to cultivate a positive mindset.

Word choice: *Joy.*

Relationship to word: *Lifts my mood.*

Mantra: *I choose joy for this day.*

Life circumstance for mantra: *Start of new day.*

Desired outcome: *Intentionally call in joy for my day.*

Word choice: _____

Relationship to word: _____

Mantra: _____

Life circumstance for mantra: _____

Desired outcome: _____

A FIRE INSIDE ME IGNITES ALL
THAT I LOVE AND BURNS AWAY
ALL THAT DOESN'T SERVE ME.

Mantra Meditation

This practice is intentional, quietly reciting pairs of mantras with each breath sequence: one mantra for the inhale and one for the exhale.

1. Create a three-word mantra for your inhale and pair it with a separate mantra for your exhale. (Example: *Inhale*—"I am peace"; *Exhale*—"I am free.")

2. Find a secluded space and position yourself however you are most comfortable.

3. Set a timer for the desired length of time.

4. Begin the meditation by taking five deep, heart-centered breaths before beginning your mantra.

5. Then, breathe with intention, reciting the pair of mantras that you prepared with each breath, in and out. You can recite the mantras aloud or to yourself.

6. You can then create additional pairs of mantras and repeat, or save the other mantras for another time and simply continue to repeat the chosen mantra pair until the timer alerts you.

7. Whenever you hear the gentle alert of the alarm, ground yourself in your body and environment with deeper breaths and gentle movements.

Gratitude is a doorway into uplifting your energy and mood. Positivity is grounded in gratitude. Take a few moments to journal about things you are grateful for. As you reflect and write, take note of how your energy feels and what thoughts of positivity might arise.

Journal about your relationship with encouragement. Reflect on how you encourage yourself and others. How do you understand encouragement? What has been the impact of your encouragement of self and others? How can you bring more encouragement as a practice in your life?

Life may be experienced in a way that feels like things might not turn out the way you hope. Journal about a time when you had to choose to hope, which felt contrary to what you were experiencing in real time. What did you gain from that experience?

_____

_____

_____

_____

_____

_____

_____

_____

_____

_____

_____

_____

_____

_____

_____

MY POSITIVITY
DOESN'T IGNORE LIFE.
MY POSITIVITY
HOLDS MY WELL-BEING.

What are some obstacles you have had to face in life? What were your thoughts about these obstacles as you faced them? How did those circumstances turn out in the end? What might be helpful ways of thinking about obstacles you may face in the future?

How do you engage in positive thinking in your relationships with others? Journal about a time someone shared something difficult with you. How did you handle it? How did what they share make you feel? How might holding space and listening be a form of positive thinking?

Both And

It's possible to recognize the challenges in life and also hold a desire to be hopeful and press on. Mindfulness is observing the moment as it is, and that includes the things you observe about yourself and your life even when they appear at odds or appear too complex. Mindfulness illuminates the present moment and creates a sense of balance mentally.

Set aside fifteen minutes to explore areas of your life, and group them into sections based on your mental observation and feelings toward each.

- Creative outlets
- Finances
- Future plans
- Goals

- Health
- Leisure
- Personal projects
- Purpose

- Relationships
- Self
- Work

POSITIVE, ENCOURAGED, HOPEFUL, CONTENT	NEUTRAL, UNCONCERNED, UNSURE, INDIFFERENT	CONCERNED, DISCOURAGED, UNSURE

Community Conversations

Conversation in community creates feelings of connectedness and an outlet for expression. The aim of this practice is to create progressive dialogue centering on each individual's personal experience with positive mindsets, vulnerability, and honesty about ideas and challenges as each relates to positivity. The focus of this practice is to generate dialogue around the idea of a positive mindset.

Take initiative in connecting with your peers, family, friends, and colleagues about the intention of this particular community conversation. Note that this community conversation practice can be used for any topic.

- Create an outline for leading a group discussion on positivity. Consider using prompts as a guide.

- Create a group chat with loved ones or initiate an in-person meetup and let them know ahead of time that the goal of the discussion is to learn from one another about their personal experiences with positive thinking.

- Take note of what others share and reflect on your own experiences with positivity in comparison.

- Journal about the feelings and energy you gain from being in the presence of others or from interacting digitally.

How do you honor the complexity of life and your changing energy and feelings along with an aim to remain positive? Do you feel it is necessary to try to remain positive even when it might feel like a challenge to do so? Why or why not?

When you commit yourself to something beyond yourself, it can create a sense of purpose. Purpose generates feelings of adequacy and hope grounded in positive energy. What are some things that you personally commit yourself to that are beyond yourself? How does this commitment make you feel?

_____

_____

_____

_____

_____

_____

_____

_____

_____

_____

_____

_____

_____

_____

_____

Giving yourself permission to say "Yes" to possibility opens up space for new opportunities. What you envision and strive toward can be a reality, and saying "Yes" to that reality is the first step. What has been your experience with saying "Yes" to possibility? How might a practice of saying "Yes" cultivate a positive mindset?

I GIVE MYSELF PERMISSION
TO EMBRACE OPTIMISM
WITHOUT APOLOGY. I PLANT
SEEDS FOR A FUTURE
THAT I DESIRE.

SECTION 5

TAKE CARE OF YOUR WHOLE SELF

Caring for yourself replenishes your personal cup. The energy you've poured out of your cup comes back to you through self-care. It is important to prioritize self-care of your whole self. This can be done through a variety of ways and will be discussed within this section. Calling all of you back to yourself is an act of self-compassion. Self-knowing and acceptance is the practice of self-awareness and gives you grace, a sense of home, and a feeling of belonging. Chasing your well-being is consistently caring for your mind and body. Resting in your wholeness brings about deep self-knowing and the ability to rest in being. Creating reminders of personal enoughness and recognizing the peace found in non-effort allows you to truly rest in being. The care of your whole self is created with intentional focus. The goal of the practices, exercises, prompts, and affirmations in this part of the journal will explore the cultivation of well-being and the care of the whole self.

I AM MY FIRST PRIORITY.
THE CARE OF MY BEING IMPACTS
HOW I CARE FOR OTHERS.

What are some ways that you engage in self-care? How often do you do things that take care of your well-being? Write down what you enjoy most in caring for yourself. Are there areas in your life where you can invite in more self-care?

Some days you might not feel like yourself. You might be feeling down or experiencing challenges. Why might it be important to still take care of yourself even when you might not be feeling your best? What are some ways you can be proactive about treating yourself well even when you are experiencing personal and life challenges?

_____

_____

_____

_____

_____

_____

_____

_____

_____

_____

_____

_____

_____

_____

_____

_____

_____

My Whole Self-Care List

Targeting the different parts of your person is helpful—emotionally, mentally, and physically. In each section, write down something you can do for yourself that will care for that particular aspect of your person. How do these different aspects of caring for yourself play into the life you create for yourself and want to live?

Emotional Care

Enjoyment: _____

Connection: _____

Release: _____

Mental Care

Relax the mind: _____

Engage the mind: _____

Teach the mind: _____

Physical Care

Exercise: _____

Relationships: _____

Rest: _____

Calming Breath Work

Being aware of your breath allows presence with various sensations of your body and activity of your mind. The calming breath work in this practice downregulates your nervous system and creates a feeling of calm. This technique can be used when feeling overwhelmed or stressed, or when you want to find inner stillness.

1. Find a quiet space and make yourself comfortable in whatever position you prefer.

2. Set a timer for ten to twenty minutes if you feel it's necessary to do so.

3. Observe your breathing. As you breathe, tap into the subtle spaces that are between your thoughts.

4. Continuing to focus on your breath, intentionally deepen the quality of your inhale and exhale. (It's important to note that your focus here is the natural rhythms of how you specifically breathe.)

5. Begin to concentrate on your inhale. When you reach capacity, hold before exhaling for as long as feels natural.

6. As you do, concentrate on your exhale. Exhale completely and wait before inhaling for as long as feels natural.

7. Repeat.

8. Stay with your practice until the timer ends or when you feel ready.

Recall a time when you took care of someone. What were the circumstances surrounding your actions? How did it feel to be able to care for someone? How does taking care of yourself impact how you are able to care for others?

_____

_____

_____

_____

_____

_____

_____

_____

_____

_____

_____

_____

_____

_____

Why is it important to forgive yourself? Can you recall a time when you forgave yourself? What did it feel like to finally come to a place where you were able to give yourself that grace? How might a practice of grace toward yourself be a way of taking care of yourself?

_____

_____

_____

_____

_____

_____

_____

_____

_____

_____

_____

_____

_____

_____

_____

_____

Define what *home* and *belonging* mean to you. What do they feel like? When was the last time you felt at home within yourself or that you were welcoming and embracing of all of you? Why might the care of yourself be connected to the sense of belonging and home you bring to yourself?

_____

_____

_____

_____

_____

_____

_____

_____

_____

_____

_____

_____

_____

_____

_____

I WILL BE INTENTIONAL
ABOUT CARING FOR
MY WELL-BEING AND ALWAYS
MAKE ROOM FOR MYSELF.

Self-awareness and acceptance create space for your own sense of home and belonging. Mindfulness of the different parts of your being and acceptance of the various things that make you who you are make up self-awareness. How can you make room for more self-awareness and acceptance in your life?

_____

_____

_____

_____

_____

_____

_____

_____

_____

_____

_____

_____

_____

_____

_____

You may give yourself and your energy away in different things you choose to undertake. This is also a reflection of your capacity. Sometimes your capacity can diminish or even be limited. What are some ways in which you determine how much capacity you have to give to a particular endeavor?

My Self-Care Calendar

Intentionally planning out the ways in which you care for yourself is one step that can be taken for personal well-being. Create a calendar of things that you would like to accomplish in the care of yourself over the next seven days. Start with whole care that you can accomplish now and build toward whole care that you can accomplish in the future.

Day 1: _____

Day 2: _____

Day 3: _____

Day 4: _____

Day 5: _____

Day 6: _____

Day 7: _____

MY SELF-CARE IS
MY BECOMING. I TRUST
THE GOOD THAT I
CREATE FOR MYSELF.

Self-Massage

Massages release tension in the body and allow for comfort and relaxation. In self-guided massages, your intuition leads you to the parts of your body that call for attention and care. Your hands move carefully and mindfully to the places you are led to rub deeply with intention.

1. Sit comfortably with your head above your heart.

2. Notice the energy of subtle sensations of your body. Breathe into how you are feeling and honor whatever is present.

3. Begin your massage by placing the back of one hand in the palm of the other. Use your thumb to massage the inner palm of your top hand, working your way around your wrist and entire hand.

4. Switch hands and repeat.

5. From your seated position, if you are able, bring the soles of your feet into both hands, begin to knead the bottoms, tops, and heels of your feet.

6. Use your intuition to guide you as to where to massage next. No matter the order in which you feel called to do this, remember to massage each limb, your stomach, the portions of your back that you can reach, and especially your head.

7. Breathe smoothly and consistently with each subtle transition to the various areas of your body.

8. Show yourself love, finishing by giving yourself a hug.

With the energy you give away, there needs to be a way to refill your personal cup, restoring and filling up your capacity to give whenever you feel the desire to give again. Journal about ways in the past you refilled your personal cup.

Was there a time when you did not pay attention to your capacity when giving of yourself? What did that feel like? Why is it important to recognize your capacity to give? What are some ways in which you have established personal boundaries in the past, and how can you ensure you honor your boundaries in the future?

Developing a consistent routine that ensures you are being proactive about your mental, emotional, and physical health is key to taking care of your whole self. What are some ways in which you have been consistent in the past about taking care of yourself? What are ways in which you can invite more consistency in whole self-care moving forward?

THERE IS NO PART OF ME
THAT I DO NOT LOVE
OR ACCEPT.

Can you recall a time in your life when you weren't consistent in self-care? Why do you think you might not have given yourself the care you needed at that time? What are some thought patterns and circumstances that lead to lack of self-care?

Remembering your adequacy and enoughness is self-affirming and creates a mindset of kindness and personal care. What are some ways you can remind yourself that you are adequate and enough? How is affirmation of your enoughness connected to the care of your whole self?

Whole Self-Care Survey

Questions that cause you to look deeper at life patterns, time spent, and behaviors can help you design better systems and practices for the care of your whole self. Create a list of three questions for each component of your person.

Examples of Questions:

- *What does self-care mean for me?*
- *How do I best accomplish my desire to take care of all of me?*

Emotional

1. _____

2. _____

3. _____

Mental

1. _____

2. _____

3. _____

Physical

1. _____

2. _____

3. _____

Feel and Name What You Feel

Feeling deeply and honoring those feelings are integral to emotional health. Emotional health is being able to navigate with care your behaviors, thoughts, and feelings. The aim of this practice is to bring into habit naming the waves of feelings that are experienced throughout the course of a day.

1. Set aside a day to commit to mindfulness of your feelings.

2. As you go about your day, use your mindfulness practice to be present with the moment and the space around you. Also remember to acknowledge the space within you.

3. Feel whatever you feel deeply and name it. Do you feel content and at ease? Name it and feel into it. Honor whatever you feel as valid.

4. Remember that mindfulness is being present with what is, in any given moment. Pause, notice, and become grounded in what is happening in the moment, as well as your current surroundings.

- What do you experience in your senses in relation to your environment?
- What is the quality of your feeling?
- What is the voice of your feeling?

5. Take notice of the transitions of your feelings in different states.

6. Repeat as long and as often as you desire throughout the course of your Feeling Day.

You exert effort as an extension of the hustle of life. *Non-efforting* is a state in which rest and being are active. To truly practice non-efforting, you must believe you are enough and complete in the moment without anything in particular to do. What do you feel and think when you reflect on non-efforting?

There are so many emotional, mental, and physical benefits to getting adequate sleep. States of rest are also helpful in nurturing your sense of well-being. What is your relationship with sleep and rest? Do you find it easy or a challenge to allow yourself to take time to do nothing? What can you do to improve your relationship with sleep and rest?

What does emotional care mean to you and how can you honor it? What does mental care mean to you and how can you honor it? What does physical care mean to you and how can you honor it?

_____

_____

_____

_____

_____

_____

_____

_____

_____

_____

_____

_____

_____

_____

_____

_____

_____

**MY CARE FOR MYSELF
IS A CELEBRATION OF
THE GIFT OF LIFE,
OF ALL OF ME.**

SECTION 6

STEP INTO YOUR POWER

Power is recognizing that everything that you need is within you, acknowledging that you have an inherent value and uniqueness that is nowhere else. No one else has your lived experience or knows life the way you do. Power is in awareness and self-inquiry, tools of discovering self-sufficiency, and enlightening every aspect of your whole self. Awareness is the space within you that observes every feeling, thought, and aspect of life. Self-inquiry is a practice of experiencing your mind, body, and life from this perspective. Accessing your personal power comes from being deeply honest and accepting of all of you. Moving through life knowing who you are and how you show up in the world is stepping into your power. The prompts, affirmations, exercises, and practices ahead will focus on your relationship to your power—power that is unique to you, transforms your life in every moment, shapes the world around you, and is the heartbeat of your freedom.

EVERY DAY, I ACKNOWLEDGE MY POWER WITHIN. I DISCOVER NEW WAYS IN WHICH I AM POWERFUL.

Reflect on your personal sense of value. What does it mean to you when you remember your worth? How does your sense of self-respect inform your personal value? Describe your value in your own words. How does it feel when you reflect on your value?

No one else has lived the life you lived and experienced life the way that you have. What does this uniqueness in the way you show up in life and take up space in this world mean to you? How can you both harness and celebrate your uniqueness more?

_____

_____

_____

_____

_____

_____

_____

_____

_____

_____

_____

_____

_____

_____

_____

_____

Using Your Imagination

Imagination is the power of the mind to both create and explore possibility. In the spaces below, take time to write out what you imagine for yourself as it relates to each category.

Your well-being: How do you want to feel emotionally, mentally, physically, etc.?

_____

Your relationships: What do your relationships to your family, friends, etc., look like?

_____

Your finances/resources: What do your personal resources look like?

_____

Your life expression: What does following your intuition and aspiration look like?

_____

Your work: What do your passion, hobbies, and creative processes look like?

_____

Your power in any circumstance: What does it look like to imagine yourself at ease?

_____

Ujjayi (Victorious Breath)

Ujjayi is a Sanskrit combination of words meaning "victorious breath." This breathing practice creates heat and a meditative state in the body. *Ujjayi* breath is calming to the body while also filling it with energy and vitality. The aim of this practice is to provide an alternative way to breathe that can be empowering when used throughout the course of your day.

1. Seal your lips and breathe in and out through your nose. On the exhales, constrict the muscles in the back of your throat. This will create a wavelike sound when breathing deeply this way.

2. It's important to remember to breathe with an emphasis on smooth, intentional nostril breathing.

3. Focus on breathing intentionally for about thirty seconds.

4. How does it feel in your body?

5. If you find it is something you can do comfortably, play with extending the length of time you use this breathing technique.

Self-inquiry as a practice seeks to unveil your truest self and most felt sense to uncover deep self-knowing. Write down what comes to mind when you reflect on who you are at your core, beyond what you have accomplished and what you think and feel. Simply ask and answer, "Who am I?"

Self-awareness is observation of your thoughts, feelings, senses, and life. Imagine being in an environment where you notice the conversation of people around you. This is what self-awareness is to the phenomena of your inner and outer world. What are your own experiences with self-awareness?

What does it mean for you to be accepting and honest with yourself? Why are acceptance and honesty with yourself necessary? Journal about a time in which you accepted and were honest with yourself and what that meant for you.

_____

_____

_____

_____

_____

_____

_____

_____

_____

_____

_____

_____

_____

_____

_____

IN SELF-AWARENESS,
I TRULY SEE MYSELF.
IN SELF-AWARENESS,
I AM FREE.

Self-knowing is acknowledging how you show up in the world and how you access your inner power. Journal about what it means for you to know yourself and how that relates to the power you notice. How do you use the personal power that comes from knowing who you are?

What responsibilities do you think come from your awareness of your power? How can you ensure you are living up to those responsibilities? How does your inner power relate to your relationship with others? How does your inner power relate to your relationship with life and yourself?

Inner Resources

One of the gifts of meditation is the ability to look deep within and assess what makes you who you are. By doing so, you can examine your inner world and discover aspects of your person and being. You are an entire world of resources and possibility. The aim of this exercise is for you to reflect and journal about your inner resources, to find them and open them up for further exploration for use in your everyday life.

Everything you need is already within you. Set aside fifteen uninterrupted minutes to journal about your inner resources.

Questions to guide your exploration include:

- What are some lived experiences that make you who you are today, and what are three qualities you can note because of it?

- What is the strength of these qualities?

- How can these qualities be used to shape your life and the world around you?

I EMBRACE FEARLESSNESS, CONFIDENCE, AND A DEEP KNOWING OF MY WORTH.

Relaxation Realization

Placing the body in states of deep relaxation activates the parasympathetic nervous system and creates feelings of calm. Realization in this practice is explored by scanning the body slowly and progressively while recalling specific enjoyable feelings from the past and visualizing those same felt senses in the future.

It is suggested that you access this practice through Savasana or "corpse pose" (see page 34), though you can do this practice in any body posture you find comfortable.

1. Find a quiet space where you can have uninterrupted time to yourself.

2. Set a timer for ten minutes (or longer, if you like).

3. Breathe deep, even, smooth breaths.

4. Allow yourself to soften into a comfortable shape.

5. Bring your attention to the crown of your head and hold it until you notice sensations, vibrations, or a tingly sensation present there. Continue breathing.

6. Recall a time you felt at peace. Pay specific attention to those feelings.

7. Draw your attention from the crown of your head to your face. Continue breathing and recall the feelings of joy, ease, and peace that you felt.

8. Continue your body scan, spending moments on each section of your body.

9. As you recall specific pleasant emotions, visualize future scenarios where you might experience those same feelings again.

10. When you hear the timer alert, ground yourself in your body and environment with deeper breaths and gentle movements.

Personal power allows you to create things for yourself and for others. This power of creation is a gift of life that can overcome obstacles and give birth to opportunities. How does it feel to know you have this capability within you and what are some things you can think of creating at this time?

What does stepping into your power mean to you? When you envision your power, what images come to mind? How does imagining tapping into your power feel in your mind, energy, and body? What are some causes of self-empowerment in your life?

Can you recall a time when you felt particularly self-sufficient and in alignment with your own power? What were the circumstances of your life when you experienced this empowerment? What were you able to accomplish because of it?

MY POWER BRINGS ME
HEALING AND PEACE.
MY POWER CREATES GOOD
IN MY LIFE AND IN OTHERS.

Self-awareness flows into self-empowerment. What are ways in which you can invite more self-awareness into your life? How might each of those things translate into being empowered? What are some other ways in which your self-empowerment might fuel your own self-awareness?

Think of a time in which your own empowerment helped someone else. What did it feel like to know you were helping someone from your own power? How does helping someone else affect your own personal power? Do you think the people you helped experienced a sense of their own empowerment?

The Elephant

Visualization of the elephant reflects grounding, strength, boundary, and the capacity to move through obstacles. Your navigation of obstacles might mean overcoming them or course-correcting to a different path or direction. The mindfulness aspect of this exercise is designed to examine personal and life obstacles and the inner power to face them with compassion, strength, and decisiveness.

Journal a list of things you consider obstacles within yourself and in your life. Then journal your thoughts about what can be done about them, as well as possible outcomes.

PERSONAL OBSTACLES	LIFE OBSTACLES
WHAT CAN BE DONE AND HOW?	WHAT CAN BE DONE AND HOW?
POSSIBLE OUTCOMES	POSSIBLE OUTCOMES

Sun Salutation A

This practice relieves stress and produces feelings of calm. For those that are seated, explore these same movements with your upper torso however you find comfortable. Before transitioning to each movement, take three to five even inhales and exhales.

1. Bring your feet hip width apart. Distribute the weight evenly in your feet. Lift up on your kneecaps, engage your core into your spine, and breathe smoothly and evenly.

2. Bring the palms of your hands to your heart center.

3. Lift your arms above your head, framing your ears with your biceps. Then bring your upper torso down toward your legs as much as is comfortable.

4. Bring your hands to your shins or to your thighs, and gaze ahead of you, flattening your back. Then bring your upper torso back down toward your legs.

5. Place your hands on the ground in front of you, positioning them as wide as your shoulders, and step both feet back behind you as wide as your hips. Gaze either at your navel or between your ankles (a posture known as Downward Dog).

6. Inhale, gaze ahead of you, and step your right foot in front of you. Plant your left foot (you can come down to your knee) and raise your arms to frame your ears with your biceps again, with your hips and front torso aligned and facing forward. Keep your knee directly above your ankle. Exhale and plant your hands and feet back into Downward Dog.

7. Inhale and gaze ahead of you, bringing both feet to where your hands are in your forward bend, and slowly rise to standing.

8. Repeat this sequence and lead with the opposite foot/side.

How would you describe freedom in your own words? Can you think of a time in your life when you felt moments of freedom? What did it feel like in your mind and body? How does this freedom connect to your sense of power? How might you be able to access power in freedom again?

Why is honesty with yourself necessary? Why is acceptance of yourself necessary? Write about a time when you were vulnerable with yourself or someone else about things that were personal to you. What was it like to be able to look deep within in that way?

Write a short note to a younger version of yourself about your understanding of your own personal power now. Share some insights and lessons with that younger version of yourself. How would you describe what your power is and how to best navigate the world because of it?

I AWAKEN TO ALL THAT
I AM AND ALL THAT I AM
CAPABLE OF. EVERYTHING
I NEED IS WITHIN ME.

Rest in Yourself; Celebrate You

You've poured parts of yourself and life into these pages. You put energy and attention into showing up for yourself in unique ways for the sake of your well-being. You didn't turn away from a deeper look within. You've filled these pages with reflections on who you are and acknowledgment of your pain, nurturing a positive mindset, taking care of your whole self, and living out of your power. By choosing the work of healing, you champion your ineffable value. Mapping your inner and outer world through writing is an ongoing gift.

Come back to journaling in different seasons of your life and see what you discover. Saying "Yes" to coming home to yourself again and again is your healing, and you can do this through whatever modality your heart leads you to. At each daybreak, say thank you to the Creator, to your ancestors, to your inmost self, or to nothing at all. Send gratitude out in whatever expression it comes because you have a new beginning in the gift of life.

Your inner knowing is a light and a guide. Commit to that deep knowing. Set boundaries around the things that your knowing reveals to you about life and yourself. Protect and commit to these things as a protection and a commitment to your inner peace, power, and happiness. As a Black masculine embodied person, you occupy a special and distinct place within the world. Your embrace of healing modalities is an anchor to your existence, an echo to your ancestors, a light to your communities, and instruction for those who come after you.

RESOURCES

Apps

Liberate Meditation App

The daily meditation app for us, by us. Explore meditations and talks designed for the Black experience.

Books

Be As You Are: The Teachings of Sri Ramana Maharshi edited by David Godman

Sri Ramana Maharshi was one of the most significant spiritual teachers to emerge from India during the first half of the twentieth century and remains widely admired. This collection of conversations between him and the many seekers who came to his ashram for guidance contains the essence of his teaching.

Man, Just Express Yourself! : An Interactive Planner Guide for MEN, Young and Old by James Harris

This book contains a way for men to identify goals and plans, express themselves, learn things, and keep records.

Websites

Black Emotional and Mental Health Collective (BEAM): beam.community

BEAM is a national training, movement-building, and grant-making institution that is dedicated to the healing, wellness, and liberation of Black and marginalized communities.

A Black Man's Safe Haven: safehaven.expressyourselfblackman.com

A Black Man's Safe Haven provides access to resources for personal development and community forums to foster improved self-expression and emotional intelligence.

Black Men Heal: linktr.ee/blackmenheal

Black Men Heal is a nonprofit organization helping provide access to free, quality therapy for men of color by providers of color.

Let's Talk Bruh (LTB): letstalkbruh.com

Let's Talk Bruh is a platform that creates interactive healing and learning experiences around Black masculinity and the impact of patriarchy in Black communities.

Melanin and Mental Health: melaninandmentalhealth.com

This is an easy-to-navigate directory for minorities to find clinicians who are culturally competent and dedicated to helping minority communities.

Therapy for Black Men: therapyforblackmen.org/therapists

This website provides targeted resources and a database filled with mental health professionals for Black men and boys.

REFERENCES

Introduction

"The Bwiti Tradition: All Things Bwiti and Its Relation to Iboga." *BwitiLife*. Accessed February 10, 2022. bwitilife.com/bwiti-tradition.

Section 1

Bell, Andrea L. "The Biology of Calm: How Downregulation Promotes Well-Being." *GoodTherapy*. October 27, 2016. goodtherapy.org/blog/biology-of-calm-how-downregulation-promotes-well-being-1027164.

Gao, Junling, Hang Kin Leung, Bonnie Wai Yun Wu, Stavros Skouras, and Hin Hung Sik. "The Neurophysiological Correlates Of Religious Chanting." *Scientific Reports* 9, no. 1 (March 2019): 4262. doi: 10.1038/s41598-019-40200-w.

Section 2

Church, Dawson, Garret Yount, and Audrey J. Brooks. "The Effect of Emotional Freedom Techniques on Stress Biochemistry." *Journal of Nervous and Mental Disease* 200, no. 10 (October 2012): 891–896. doi: 10.1097/NMD.0b013e31826b9fc1.

Acknowledgments

To my mother, Diedre, for your constant wisdom and love. To my father, Daniel Fluker Sr., for life lessons. To my grandfather, James Fluker Sr., for your care of our family. To Angela and Quay for believing in me. To Pedro Santos for being an ineffable light to my path. To the Bwiti Life Center and Moughenda Village for community and a living connection to my ancestral spiritual heritage. To Brandon Copeland for your patience. To Remiko for an example of divine masculinity. To Deverell for your foresight and trust. To the Black Boys OM Collective, for believing in my vision. To the Esalen Institute of Human Potential for its sacred grounds and helping me open up to my own expansiveness.

About the Author

Danny Angelo Fluker Jr. is a mindful creative and community healing advocate. He is a meditation, yoga, and mindfulness teacher, creator of Black Boys OM, speaker, and Missoko Bwiti practitioner.